BRANDON DEVONTÉ ALFRED

THE TRUTH

"Then you will know the truth, and
the truth will set you free."

-John 8:32

Contents

Preface

As a young man, I was always curious about whom GOD was and wanted to learn more about Him. I had such a strong inner desire to learn about Him that I decided to dedicate time every day to reading at least one chapter out of the Bible. In reading the various scriptures every day I felt closer to GOD and became more and more knowledgeable about His Word. I felt like a "NEW Light" had shined upon me and I enjoyed every moment that I spent reading the Bible. As my life continued I witnessed much suffering of others. I knew that if they could find their way to God's Word it would also help them to navigate through life's journey. It is my prayer, hope, and belief that reading this book will encourage, inspire and lead you to THE TRUTH.

Chapter 1

This Generation

This is what GOD says about this generation, "...You will be ever hearing but never understanding; you will be ever seeing but never perceiving. For this people's heart has become calloused; they hardly hear with their ears, and they have closed their eyes. Otherwise they might see with their eyes, hear with their ears, understand with their hearts and turn, and I (GOD) would heal them." (Acts 28: 26-27)

"Therefore, I urge you, brothers, in view of God's mercy, to offer your bodies as living sacrifices, holy and pleasing to God this is your spiritual act of worship. Do not conform any longer to the pattern of this world, but be transformed by the renewing of your mind. Then you will be able to test and approve what God's will is- his good, pleasing and perfect will. For by the grace given me I say to every one of you: Do not think of yourself more highly than you ought, but rather think of yourself with sober judgment, in accordance with the measure of faith God has given you." (Romans 12:1-3)

"Do everything without complaining or arguing, so that you may become blameless and pure, children of God without fault in a crooked and depraved generation, in which you shine like stars in the universe as you hold out the word of life…" (Philippians 2:14-16)

True Success

"Worldly Success" is measured by how much money you have in the bank. "True Success" is measured by the wisdom and knowledge that you obtained about God and how much faith you have in Him. **Wisdom** is knowledge in action and **knowledge** is wisdom. "True Success" is the result of work done in peace. All your lessons cannot be learned without difficulty. It's because God considers that our present sufferings are not worth comparing with the glory that will be revealed in us.

"GOD does not hide your righteousness in His heart; GOD speaks of your faithfulness and salvation. GOD doesn't conceal your love and your truth from the great assembly." (Psalm 40:10)

As it states in Deuteronomy 8:18 - "But remember the Lord your God, for it is he who gives you the ability to produce wealth, and so confirms his covenant, which he swore to your forefathers, as it is today."

"No one can serve two masters. Either he will hate the one and love the other, or he will be devoted to the one and despise the other. You cannot serve both God and Money." (Matthew 6:24)

"Now listen, you who say, 'Today or tomorrow we will go to this or that city, spend a year there, carry on business and make money.' Why, you do not even know what will happen tomorrow. What is your life? You are a mist that appears for a little while and then vanishes. Instead, you ought to say, 'If it is the Lord's will, we will live and do this or that.' As it is, you boast and brag. All such boasting is evil. Anyone, then, who knows the good he ought to do and he doesn't do it, sins." (James 4:13-17)

As it states in Proverbs 3:27-28 – "Do not withhold good from those who deserve it, when it is in your power to act. Do not say to your neighbor, 'Come back later; I'll give it tomorrow' – when you now have it with you."

The Word goes on to say in 1 Timothy 6:17-18 - "Command those who are rich in this present world not to be arrogant nor to put their hope in wealth, which is so uncertain, but to put their hope in God, who richly provides us with everything for our enjoyment. Command them to do good, to be rich in good deeds, and to be generous and willing to share."

Revelation 3:17 states "You say, 'I am rich; I have acquired wealth and do not need a thing.' But you do not realize that you are wretched, pitiful, poor, blind and naked."

Unless you open the door for Jesus to come in, you have obtained nothing meaningful or beneficial. You have to let the LORD GOD be your provider and Savior. Listen to the LORD GOD and the Holy Spirit that lives inside of you. Do not be cocky or arrogant, but humble and giving.

As it reads in James 1:9-11 - "The brother in humble circumstances ought to take pride in his high position. But the one who is rich should take pride in his low position, because he will pass away like a wild flower. For the sun rises with scorching heat and withers the plant; its blossom falls and its beauty is destroyed. In the same way, the rich man will fade away even while he goes about his business."

It further reads in Philippians 2:3 & 4 – "Do nothing out of selfish ambition or vain conceit, but in humility consider others better than yourselves. Each of you should look not only to your own interests, but also to the interests of others."

"...Remembering the words the Lord Jesus himself said: 'It is more blessed to give than to receive." (Acts 20:35) For "Wealth" is but an earthly metaphor for "Power" that only the LORD GOD has.

True Church

The "True Church" is not the one made of brick or mortar, but the one of the Holy Spirit. Ministers of the "True Church" do not peddle The Word of GOD for profit, unlike so many. You don't have to sit in a building on a certain day or at a certain hour...you can have church in the comfort of your own home (Early Church). I believe we have lost sight of the fact that we are supposed to be the "True Church," which is MUCH BIGGER than a man-made building. Too often individuals attend the man-made sanctuary and go through the motions of "just being there" and leave just as messed up as they were when they went into the structure.

The True Sabbath is on the seventh day which is a Saturday, not a so-called Sunday. "...And on the seventh day God rested from all his work." (Hebrews 4:4)

You can praise GOD wherever and whenever you want. GOD doesn't want to force somebody to love and know about Him...He wants he or she to want to know more about Him and love Him wholeheartedly, so there will be no restraint between GOD and you. Then that's when the Holy Spirit takes control. In order to remain in God's presence you don't have to stay in a church (building), but make your heart a chapel where you can go any time to talk to GOD privately. ***Faith comes by hearing the message and the message is heard through the Word of Christ.*** Then the understanding will be given once the Holy Spirit is received by you.

"...Be shepherds of the church of God (True Church), which he bought with his own blood." (Acts 20:28)

There will be people out there, that will come among you and try to distort the "Truth," but you have to be strong. Just keep on committing to GOD and to His Word, which can build you up and give you an inheritance among all those who are sanctified. (Acts 20:32)

As it states in Luke 10:2 – "...The harvest is plentiful, but the workers are few."

The LORD Is Your Refuge

Many may say "GOD will not deliver you." But you must know that GOD is a shield around you and He will bestow glory on you and lift up your head. From the LORD comes deliverance. "Consider it pure joy, my brothers, whenever you face trials of many kinds, because you know that the testing of your faith develops perseverance. Perseverance must finish its work so that you may be mature and complete, not lacking anything." (James 1:2-4)

"Blessed is the man who perseveres under trial, because when he has stood the test, he will receive the crown of life that God has promised to those who love him." (James 1:12)

Thus, "In your anger do not sin; when you are on your beds, search your hearts and be silent." (Psalm 4:4)

Trust in the LORD GOD your one and only Savior. Lie down and sleep in peace for the LORD GOD will keep you in safety.

As it states in Psalm 46:1-2 - "God is our refuge and strength, an ever-present help in trouble. Therefore we will not fear..."

"If you make the Most High your dwelling – even the Lord, who is my refuge – then no harm will befall you, no disaster will come near your tent. For he will command his angels concerning you to guard you in all your ways..." (Psalm 91:9-11)

"Because he loves me, says the Lord, I will rescue him; I will protect him, for he acknowledges my name. He will call upon me, and I will answer him; I will be with him in trouble, I will deliver him and honor him. With long life will I satisfy him and show him my salvation." (Psalm 91:14-16)

"For surely GOD is your salvation you will trust and not be afraid. For the LORD is your strength and your song." (Isaiah 12:2)

Then you will say of the LORD, "He is my refuge and my fortress, my GOD, in whom I trust." (Psalm 91:2)

"I lift up my eyes to the hills – where does my help come from? My help comes from the Lord, the Maker of heaven and earth. He will not let our foot slip – he who watches over you will not slumber; indeed, he who watches over Israel will neither slumber nor sleep. The Lord watches over you – the Lord is your shade at your right hand; the sun will not harm you by day, nor the moon by night. The Lord will keep you from all harm – he will watch over your life; the Lord will watch over your coming and going both now and forevermore." (Psalm 121:1-8)

"Be still, and know that I am God..." (Psalm 46:10)

Spiritual Gifts

Do not be ignorant of your spiritual gifts, because when you were pagans you were led away to worship mute idols. (1 Corinthians 12:1-2)

"There are different kinds of gifts, but the same Spirit. There are different kinds of service, but the same Lord. There are different kinds of working, but the same God works all of them in all men. Now to each one the manifestation of the Spirit is given for the common good. To one there is given through the Spirit the message of wisdom, to another the message of knowledge by means of the same Spirit, to another faith by the same Spirit, to another gifts of healing by that one Spirit, to another miraculous powers, to another prophecy, to another distinguishing between spirits, to another speaking in different kinds of tongues, and to still another the interpretation of tongues. All these are the work of one and the same Spirit, and he gives them to each one, just as he determines." (1 Corinthians 12:4-11)

Therefore, do not lack any spiritual gift as you eagerly wait for the Lord Jesus Christ to be revealed.

As it states in Ephesians 4:11-16 – "It was he who gave some to be apostles, some to be prophets, some to be evangelists, and some to be pastors and teachers, to prepare God's people for works of service, so that the body of Christ may be built up until we all reach unity in faith and in the knowledge of the Son of God and become mature, attaining to the whole measure of the fullness of Christ. Then we will no longer be infants, tossed back and forth by the waves, and blown here and there by every wind of teaching and by the cunning and craftiness of men in their deceitful scheming. Instead, speaking the truth in love, we will in all things grow up into him who is the Head, that is, Christ. From him the whole body, joined and held together by every supporting ligament, grows and builds itself up in love, as each part does it work."

"For God did not give us a spirit of timidity, but a spirit of power, of love and of self-discipline." (2 Timothy 1:7)

Being a Servant of the LORD GOD

"You were taught, with regard to your former way of life, to put off your old self, which is being corrupted by its deceitful desires; to be made new in the attitude of your minds; and to put on the new self, created to be like God in true righteousness and holiness." (Ephesians 4:22-26)

When you fast, do not let everyone see you fasting. Only let your Father in Heaven see what you do in secret. Then He will reward you for what you have done in secret. (Matthew 6:17-18)

Each of you must put off falsehood and speak trustfully to his neighbor, for we are all members of the Body of Christ. In your anger do not sin.

For it reads in Proverbs 3:29-35 – "Do not plot against your neighbor, who lives trustfully near you. Do not accuse a man for no reason – when he has done you no harm. Do not envy a violent man or choose any of his ways, for the Lord detests a perverse man but takes the upright into his confidence. The Lord's curse is on the house of the wicked, but he blesses the home of the righteous. He mocks proud mockers but gives grace to the humble. The wise inherit honor, but fools he holds up to shame."

It further reads in Ephesians 4:29 and Ephesians 4:31-32 – "Do not let any unwholesome talk come out of your mouths, but only what is helpful for building others up according to their needs, that it may benefit those who listen."

".....Get rid of all bitterness, rage and anger, brawling and slander, along with every form of malice. Be kind and compassionate to one another, forgiving each other, just as in Christ God forgave you."

It states in Titus 3:9 – "But avoid foolish controversies and genealogies and arguments and quarrels about the law, because these are unprofitable and useless."

"But among you there must not be even a hint of sexual immorality, or of any kind of impurity, or of greed, because these are improper for God's holy people. Nor should there be obscenity, foolish talk or coarse joking, which are out of place, but rather thanksgiving. For of this you can be sure: No immoral, impure or greedy person – such a man is an idolater – has an inheritance in the kingdom of Christ and of God." (Ephesians 5: 3-5)

"Be very careful, then, how you live – not as unwise but as wise, making the most of every opportunity, because the days are evil. Therefore do not be foolish, but understand what the Lord's will is. Do not get drunk on wine, which leads to debauchery. Instead, be filled with the Spirit." (Ephesians 5:15-18)

"Teach the older men to be temperate, worthy of respect, self-controlled, and sound in faith, in love and in endurance. Likewise, teach the older women to be reverent in the way they live, not to be slanderers or addicted to much wine, but to teach what is good. Then they can train the younger women (if they choose to get married & have children), to love their husbands and children, to be self-controlled and pure, to be busy at home, to be kind, and to be subject to their husbands, so that no one will malign the word of God. Similarly, encourage the young men to be self-controlled. In everything set them an example by doing what is good. In your teaching show integrity, seriousness and soundness of speech that cannot be condemned, so that those who oppose you may be ashamed because they have nothing bad to say about us (God and you)." (Titus 2:2-8)

"Speak to one another with psalms, hymns and spiritual songs. Sing and make music in your heart to the Lord, always giving thanks to God the Father for everything, in the name of our Lord Jesus Christ. Submit to one another out of reverence for Christ." (Ephesians 5:19-21)

"Is it not to share your food with the hungry and to provide the poor wanderer with shelter – when you see the naked, to clothe him, and not to turn away from your own flesh and blood? Then your light will break forth like the dawn, and your healing will quickly appear; then your righteousness will go before you, and the glory of the Lord will be your rear guard." (Isaiah 58:7-8)

"When you see a wicked man and you know that God will not spare him because of all his wicked acts, yet you do not even try to dissuade him from his sin, God will hold you accountable for his blood. But, if you do warn the wicked man to turn from his ways and he does not do so, he will die for his sin, but you will have saved yourself." (Ezekiel 33:8-9)

"Warn a divisive person once, and then warn him a second time. After that, have nothing to do with him. You may be sure that such a man is warped and sinful; he is self-condemned." (Titus 3:10-11)

"If a righteous man turns from his righteousness and does evil, he will die for it. And if a wicked man turns away from his wickedness and does what is just and right, he will live by doing so." (Ezekiel 33:18-19)

"But you, dear friends, build yourselves up in your most holy faith and pray in the Holy Spirit. Keep yourselves in God's love as you wait for the mercy of our Lord Jesus Christ to bring you to eternal life. Be merciful to those who doubt; snatch others from the fire and save them; to others show mercy, mixed with fear – hating even the clothing stained by corrupted flesh." (Jude 1:20-23)

Act justly, love mercifully, and walk humbly with Our God.

"Finally, be strong in the Lord and in his mighty power. Put on the full armor of God so that you can take your stand against the devil's schemes. For our struggle is not against flesh and blood, but against the rulers, against the authorities, against the powers of this dark world and against the spiritual forces of evil in the heavenly realms. Therefore put on the full armor of God, so that when the day of evil comes, you may be able to stand your ground, and after you have done everything, to stand. Stand firm then, with the belt of truth buckled around your waist, with the breastplate of righteousness in place and with your feet fitted with the readiness that comes from the gospel of peace. In addition to all this, take up the shield of faith, with which you can extinguish all the flaming arrows of the evil one. Take the helmet of salvation and the sword of the Spirit, which is the word of God. And pray in the Spirit on all occasions with all kinds of prayers and requests...." (Ephesians 6:10-18)

"Remind the people to be subject to rulers and authorities, to be obedient, to be ready to do whatever is good, to slander no one, to be peaceable and considerate, and to show true humility toward all men. At one time we too were foolish, disobedient, deceived and enslaved by all kinds of passions and pleasures. We lived in malice and envy, being hated and hating one another. But when the kindness and love of God our Savior appeared, he saved us, not because of righteous things we had done, but because of his mercy. He saved us through the washing of rebirth and renewal by the Holy Spirit, whom he poured out on us generously through Jesus Christ our Savior, so that, having been justified by his grace, we might become heirs having the hope of eternal life." (Titus 3: 1-7)

"God had planned something better for us so that only together with us would they be made perfect." (Hebrews 11:40)

"Praise the Lord. Blessed is the man who fears the Lord, who finds great delight in his commands. His children will be mighty in the land; the generation of the upright will be blessed. Wealth and riches are in his house, and his righteousness endures forever. Even in the darkness light dawns for the upright, for the gracious and compassionate and righteous man. Good will come to him who is generous and lends freely, who conducts his affairs with justice. Surely he will never be shaken; a righteous man will be remembered forever. He will have no fear of bad news; his heart is steadfast, trusting in the Lord. His heart is secure, he will have no fear; in the end he will look in triumph on his foes. He has scattered abroad his gifts to the poor, his righteousness endures forever; his horn will be lifted high in honor." (Psalm 112: 1-9)

"Always remember my fellow brothers and sisters in Christ that the one who sows to please the Spirit, from the Spirit will reap eternal life. Let us not become weary in doing good, for at the proper time we will reap a harvest if we do not give up. Therefore, as we have opportunity, let us do good to all people, especially to those who belong to the family of believers." (Galatians 6:8-10)

It states in Psalms 1:1-3 - "Blessed is the man who does not walk in the counsel of the wicked or stand in the way of sinners or sit in the seat of mockers. But his delight is in the law of the Lord, and on his law he meditates day and night. He is like a tree planted by streams of water, which yields its fruit in season and whose leaf does not wither. Whatever he does prospers."

"...So restrain your voice from weeping and your eyes from tears, for your work will be rewarded." (Jeremiah 31:16)

"For we are God's workmanship, created in Christ Jesus to do good works, which God prepared in advance for us to do." (Ephesians 2:10)

"...Live in peace with each other.....warn those who are idle, encourage the timid, help the weak, be patient with everyone. Make sure that nobody pays back wrong for wrong, but always try to be kind to each other and to everyone else. Be joyful always; pray continually; give thanks in all circumstances, for this is God's will for you in Christ Jesus. Do not put out the Spirit's fire; do not treat prophecies with contempt. Test everything.

Hold on to the good. Avoid every kind of evil. May God himself, the God of peace, sanctify you through and through. May your whole spirit, soul and body be kept blameless at the coming of our Lord Jesus Christ. The one who calls you is faithful and he will do it." (1 Thessalonians 5:13-24)

As it states in Jeremiah 29:11-13 - "'For I know the plans I have for you,' declares the Lord, 'plans to prosper you and not to harm you, plans to give you hope and a future. Then you will call upon me and come and pray to me, and I will listen to you. You will seek me and find me when you seek me with all your heart...'"

Chapter 2

Loving One Another

"Love must be sincere. Hate what is evil; cling to what is good. Be devoted to one another in brotherly love. Honor one another above yourselves. Never be lacking in zeal, but keep your spiritual fervor, serving the Lord. Be joyful in hope, patient in affliction, faithful in prayer. Share with God's people who are in need. Practice hospitality." (Romans 12:9-13)

"If you have material possessions and see a brother in need and have no pity on him, how can the love of God be in you? For let us not love with words or tongue but with actions and in truth. This then is how you know that you belong to the truth, and how you set your hearts at rest in God's presence whenever your hearts condemn you. For God is greater than your heart, and He knows everything. So dear friends, if your heart does not condemn you, you have confidence before God and receive from Him anything you ask, because you obey His commands and do what pleases Him. And this is His command: to believe in the name of His Son, Jesus Christ, and to love one another as He commanded us. Also to love the Lord your God with all your heart, with all your soul, with all your mind and all your strength. Those who obey His commands live in

Him, and He in them. And this is how we know that He lives in us: We know it by the Spirit He gave us." (1 John 3:17-24)

Maybe you have heard, "Love your neighbor as yourself," but I tell you "Love your enemies as if they were your true family." Pray for those who persecute you. (Matthew 5:43-44)

As it states in Matthew 5:46-48 – "If you love those who love you, what reward will you get? …. And if you greet only your brothers, what are you doing more than others? …. Be perfect, therefore, as your heavenly Father is perfect."

"Bless those who persecute you; bless and do not curse. Rejoice with those who rejoice; mourn with those who mourn. Live in harmony with one another. Do not be proud, but be willing to associate with people of low position. Do not be conceited. Do not repay anyone evil for evil. Be careful to do what is right in the eyes of everybody. If it is possible, as far as it depends on you, live at peace with everyone. Do not take revenge, my friends, but leave room for God's wrath, for it is written: 'It is mine to avenge; I will repay, says the Lord." (Romans 12:14-19)

It further reads in Romans 12:21 – "Do not be overcome by evil, but overcome evil with good."

Always be ready to give, not receive. When you do give, give generously... not expecting anything back...for GOD knows when it is done out of your heart. When you give from your heart, GOD will bless you a hundred fold for being that Angel. Remember you make a living by what you get, but you make a life by what you give. So do to others what you would have them do to you. For you must have "love" to please GOD.

"Love is patient, love is kind. It does not envy, it does not boast, it is not proud. It is not rude, it is not self-seeking, it is not easily angered, it keeps no record of wrongs. Love does not delight in evil but rejoices with the truth. It always protects, always trusts, always hopes, always perseveres. Love never fails....." (1 Corinthians 13:4-8)

"If you obey the Lord's commands, you will remain in the Lord's love, just as Jesus had obeyed His Father's commands and so remains in His love. You have been told this so that the Lord's joy may be in you and that your joy may be complete. The Lord's command is this: Love each other as I have loved you. For greater love has no one than this, that he lay down his life for his friends. You are a friend of the Lord if you do what He commands. The Lord no longer calls you servants, because a servant does not know his master's business. Instead, He has called you friends, for everything that Jesus has learned from His Father, Jesus has made known to you. You did not choose the Lord, but the Lord chose you and appointed you to go and bear fruit – fruit that will last. Then the Father will give you whatever you ask in Jesus' name. This is the Lord's command: Love each other." (John 15:10-17)

To Have Your Conscience Clear: "Do Not Worry" (Matthew 6)

"You have to care very little if you are judged by a person or by a human court; indeed, you must not even judge yourself. Then your conscience is clear, but that does not make you innocent. It is the Lord who judges you. Therefore judge nothing before the appointed time; wait till the Lord comes. He will bring to light what is hidden in darkness and will expose the motives of men's hearts. At that time each will receive his praise from God." (1 Corinthians 4:3-5)

"Now faith is being sure of what we hope for and certain of what we do not see......And without faith it is impossible to please God, because anyone who comes to him must believe that he exists and that he rewards those who earnestly seek him.....God had planned something better for us so that only together with us would they be made perfect." (Hebrew 11:1, 6 & 40)

"So we make it our goal to please him, whether we are at home in the body or away from it. For we must all appear before the judgment seat of Christ, that each one may receive what is due him for the things done while in the body, whether good or bad." (2 Corinthians 5:9-10)

Then when you have been justified through faith, you will have peace with God through our Lord Jesus Christ and your conscience will be clear. Remember the Lord's perfect peace takes away all concerns and fear. When you are concerned, then you do not trust the Lord to take care of you or your loved one. You think of all the worse things that can happen. All that is, is the devil trying to get into your head. For example, you have a goal, and then a problem presents itself. You do not have to think about the problem...you can just keep on going unafraid, trusting in Our Lord and Savior Jesus Christ.

If you do look at the problem and concentrate on it long enough, your dream of getting to that goal will be delayed. You see "Fear" is the devil in disguise. So don't let the devil stop what GOD has in store for you. Remember speak positively, not negatively...for example using the word "worry" is a negative stressor. For the difficulties of life are caused by disharmony in the individual.

Judging (Stereotype & Racism)

"Do not judge or you too will be judged. For in the same way you judge others, you will be judged, and with the measure you use, it will be measured to you." (Matthew 7:1-2)

"You, therefore, have no excuse, you who pass judgment on someone else, for at whatever point you judge the other, you are condemning yourself, because you who pass judgment do the same things." (Romans 2:1)

Accept one another for who they are...for as Martin Luther King Jr. said, "Stop judging people based on the color of one's skin, but by the content of their character." Stop trying to see with your eyes, but look with your heart.

For example, a Black person and a Mexican person could have everything in common, but society wouldn't agree with that because society thinks that you should always stick with your race. But you have to see that color does not have to affect who you like or what you have in common with anybody, whether you are Black, White, Mexican, Asian, Indian, Bi-racial or Multiracial, etc. So if you are not Black (let's pretend for a moment that you are) and live in a Black community...although you are Black, you still may not feel any "brotherly" connection. It is in this case that society makes you feel like an outsider or an outcast. Now let us say that this Black individual is now placed in a Mexican community, and feels some kind of connection with those in this community. In this instance this individual may feel so connected with this group of people, that the feeling that they should have been born brothers, could emerge. The feeling of closeness can be so real that they would be able to "take a bullet" or die for one another.

Let us suppose now that there is a girl in a biracial romantic relationship. She breaks up because society views that two different races should not be together or be friends. But, both of them shouldn't stop being a couple or being friends because "color" is just "a color." What people need to get across in their minds is that the color of one's skin is just "a color" and it does not determine how smart or ignorant one is or the way one cooks, acts, dresses, behaves, talks, and even how one walks. Don't link other people together because of the color of their skin. Everybody is a human being and has his or her own style and personality. Every human being acts differently in their own unique way and God is the only one who can judge.

True Wisdom

The wisdom GOD gives you is better than silver or gold. "If any of you lacks wisdom, he should ask God, who gives generously to all without finding fault, and it will be given to him. But when he asks, he must believe and not doubt, because he who doubts is like a wave of the sea, blown and tossed by the wind. That man should not think he will receive anything from the Lord; he is a double-minded man, unstable in all he does." (James 1:5-8)

"Do not merely listen to the word, and so deceive yourselves. Do what it says." (James 1:22)

"Wisdom" is a gift of God. When you receive His wisdom, that is the gift of His Love. You can be given "wisdom" at a young age...age means nothing. You may think that "Age should speak; advanced years should teach wisdom. But it is the spirit in a man, the breath of the Almighty, that gives him understanding. It is not only the old who are wise, not only the aged who understand what is right." (Job 32:6-9)

In the book entitled, **_Today God Says_ by Clift Richards with Lloyd Hildebrand** it reads: "...wisdom and happiness are inseparable, I can't have one without the other." **_Today God Says_** also shares with us that "The joy of the Lord is not a fickle emotion that is based on the circumstance I'm experiencing; rather, it is an abiding happiness that comes from the knowledge that God has everything under control." One must be knowledgeable that even though an education can be paid for, it does not necessarily result in wisdom.

Relationships

If a relationship is going to last to the end of time, GOD must be the center of the relationship, the MOST IMPORTANT aspect in both lives. It can't be for show or just to get attention. It has to be both people that love GOD and each other so much that they will wait until they get married to have intercourse with one another. It's because the relationship would not be on a physical level, it would be on a higher level - "A Spiritual Level."

"An unmarried man is concerned about the Lord's affairs – how he can please the Lord. But a married man is concerned about the affairs of this world – how he can please his wife – and his interests are divided. An unmarried woman or virgin is concerned about the Lord's affairs: Her aim is to be devoted to the Lord in both body and spirit. But a married woman is concerned about the affairs of this world – how she can please her husband. I am saying this for your own good, not to restrict you, but that you may live in a right way in undivided devotion to the Lord." (1 Corinthians 7:32-35)

Nevertheless, each one of us should retain the place in life that the Lord has assigned to him or her and to which GOD has called him or her to do.

"Wives, submit to your husbands as to the Lord. For the husband is the head of the wife as Christ is the head of the church, his body, of which he is the Savior. Now as the church submits to Christ, so also wives should submit to their husbands in everything. Husbands, love your wives, just as Christ loved the church and gave himself up for her to make her holy, cleansing her by the washing with water through the word, and to present her to himself as a radiant church, without stain or wrinkle or any other blemish, but holy and blameless. In this same way, husbands ought to love their wives as their own bodies. He who loves his wife loves himself." (Ephesians 5:22-28)

It further states in Ephesians 6:4 - "Fathers, do not exasperate your children; instead, bring them up in the training and instruction of the Lord."

Chapter 3

Do Not Be Yoked With Unbelievers

"Do you not know that he who unites himself with a prostitute is one with her in body? For it is said, 'The two will become one flesh.' But he who unites himself with the Lord is one with him in spirit." (1 Corinthians 6:16-17)

"Do not be yoked together with unbelievers. For what do righteousness and wickedness have in common? Or what fellowship can light have with darkness?" (2 Corinthians 6:14)

"What agreement is there between the temple of God and idols? For we are the temple of the living God. As God has said: I will live with them and walk among them, and I will be their God, and they will be my people. Therefore come out from them and be separate, says the Lord. Touch no unclean thing, and I will receive you. I will be a Father to you, and you will be my sons and daughters, says the Lord Almighty." (2 Corinthians 6:16-18)

It further reads in 2 Corinthians 7:1 – "Since we have these promises, dear friends, let us purify ourselves from everything that contaminates body and spirit, perfecting holiness out of reverence for God."

Be careful not to be a person who knows GOD, but doesn't glorify Him. It states in Romans 1:21-25 - "For although they knew God, they neither glorified him as God nor gave thanks to him, but their thinking became futile and their foolish hearts were darkened. Although they claimed to be wise, they became fools and exchanged the glory of the immortal God for images made to look like mortal man and birds and animals and reptiles. Therefore God gave them over in the sinful desires of their hearts to sexual impurity for the degrading of their bodies with one another. They exchanged the truth of God for a lie, and worshiped and served created things rather than the Creator – who is forever praised. Amen."

"Let no one deceive you with empty words, for because of such things God's wrath comes on those who are disobedient. Therefore do not be partners with them. For you were once darkness, but now you are light in the Lord. Live as children of light (for the fruit of the light consists in all goodness, righteousness and truth) and find out what pleases the Lord. Have nothing to do with the fruitless deeds of darkness, but rather expose them. For it is shameful even to mention what the disobedient do in secret. But everything exposed by the light becomes visible, for it is light that makes everything visible. This is why it is said: 'Wake up, O sleeper, rise from the dead, and Christ will shine on you.' Be very careful, then, how you live – not as unwise but as wise, making the most of every opportunity, because the days are evil. Therefore do not be foolish, but understand what the Lord's will is. Do not get drunk on wine, which leads to debauchery. Instead, be filled with the Spirit. Speak to one another with psalms, hymns and spiritual songs. Sing and make music in your heart to the Lord, always giving thanks to God the Father for everything, in the name of our Lord Jesus Christ. Submit to one another out of reverence for Christ."(Ephesians 5:6-21)

Jealousy, Anger, Murder, Oath's, Tooth for Tooth & False Sheep

You see people enjoy and thrive off of other people's jealousy and anger. The feeling they get from jealousy and anger is called "evil happiness." If you thrive off of "evil happiness" you become so use to it, and then when all the jealousy and anger stops, you become nothing but an empty soul. It's because that was your energy, what you desired from people to keep you going every day, to keep you from not feeling pain for that moment.

Also, when you murder, it is only the devil possessing you. A way that you can drive out the devil is by saying, "I rebuke you Satan in Jesus Name." Get all that jealousy and anger out of you. Get an object to squeeze or snap if you start to anger fast. If you do that, then you will become more peaceful and killing somebody would not even be on your mind. You see, the only thing the devil can control is your mind, if you let him. But, when you are at peace and you settle matters with everyone, GOD will take control.

Remember when you make a promise or an oath, "Simply let your 'Yes' be 'Yes' and your 'No' be 'No'; anything beyond this comes from the evil one." (Matthew 5:37)

If an evil person comes in your pathway resist him or her. Just simply ignore he or she and go on with your GOD-Purpose day. For the devil does not know if he is annoying you until you pay him the slightest bit of attention. If it is continuous, pray to GOD to give you the strength not to explode. Ask your Father which is in Heaven to take care of that person, for it is not your battle to fight.

If someone talks bad about you pray for them, turn and walk away with a peaceful smile. If a person hits you or attacks you purposely out of anger (not friendly) and you know it's on purpose...Ask yourself what would Jesus do, and then ask GOD for guidance.

"Give to the one who asks you, and do not turn away from the one who wants to borrow from you." (Matthew 5:42)

Watch out for the many false sheep out in the world today. Now there might be people who are preaching out there saying, "LORD, I love you and praise your Holy name"...with their mouths they bless, but in their hearts they curse. God's true sheep are the people who do the will of GOD in Heaven, not the will of the fleshly heart.

"I urge you, brothers, to watch out for those who cause division and put obstacles in your way that are contrary to the teaching you have learned. Keep away from them. For such people are not serving our Lord Christ, but their own appetites. By smooth talk and flattery they deceive the minds of naive people." (Romans 16:17-18)

"These people honor me with their lips, but their hearts are far from me. They worship me in vain; their teachings are but rules taught by men." (Matthew 15:8-9)

"For there are many rebellious people, mere talkers and deceivers, especially those of the circumcision group. They must be silenced, because they are ruining whole households by teaching things they ought not to teach – and that for the sake of dishonest gain. Even one of their own prophets has said, 'Cretans are always liars, evil brutes, lazy gluttons.' This testimony is true. Therefore, rebuke them sharply, so that they will be sound in the faith and pay no attention to the Jewish myths or to the commands of those who reject the truth. To the pure, all things are pure, but to those who are corrupted and do not believe, nothing is pure. In fact, both their minds and consciences are corrupted. They claim to know God, but by their actions they deny him. They are detestable, disobedient and unfit for doing anything good." (Titus 1:10-16)

Struggling with Sin but Having A Choice

The way you keep away from looking at the opposite sex lustfully is to simply stay close to GOD. Let the love of GOD be in your heart, not evil. So, if you do look at the opposite sex lustfully, you haven't let GOD take over your heart and soul.

"........The body is not meant for sexual immorality, but for the Lord, and the Lord for the body." (1 Corinthians 6:13) "Do you not know that your body is a temple of the Holy Spirit, who is in you, whom you have received from God? You are not your own; you were bought at a price. Therefore honor God with your body." (1 Corinthians 6:19 & 20)

When temptation comes your way and you want to have intercourse with the opposite sex and you're not married, always know that you can stop yourself, because GOD does not give you more than you can handle. If you do give into temptation it's because you are weak or you just weren't trying hard enough! You have to pray to GOD and repent and ask for forgiveness from the bottom of your heart. This needs to be done each and every day and when you do, you will become stronger in resisting the devil's schemes to destroy you.

If you are a person that desires to do good, but cannot carry out; "then you keep on doing the evil you do not want to do, it is no longer you who do it, but it is the sin living in you that does it." (Romans 7:19- 20)

So what is happening is that ..."when you want to do good, evil is right there with you. For in your inner being you delight in God's Law, but you see another law at work in the members of your body, waging war against the law of your mind and making you think that you are a prisoner of the law of sin at work within your members." (Romans 7:21-23)

Do not be a prisoner of your mind, let your heart be your guide. You must already know that God has given you the key to unlock the cell you are in and be set free. God sometimes lets us go through struggles so we can straighten out what was left unfinished.

"In the same way, count yourselves dead to sin but alive to God in Christ Jesus. Therefore do not let sin reign in your mortal body so that you obey its evil desires. Do not offer the parts of your body to sin, as instruments of wickedness, but rather offer yourselves to God, as those who have been brought from death to life; and offer the parts of your body to him as instruments of righteousness. For sin shall not be your master, because you are not under law, but under grace." (Romans 6:11-14)

"For the grace of God that brings salvation has appeared to all men. It teaches us to say 'No' to ungodliness and worldly passions, and to live self controlled, upright and godly lives in this present age, while we wait for the blessed hope – the glorious reappearance of our great God and Savior, Jesus Christ, who gave himself for us to redeem us from all wickedness and to purify for himself a people that are his very own, eager to do what is good." (Titus 2: 11-14)

"To him who overcomes, Jesus will give the right to sit with Him on His throne, just as Jesus overcame and sat down with His Father on His throne." (Revelation 3:21)

"You were taught, with regard to your former way of life, which is being corrupted by its deceitful desires; to be made new in the attitude of your minds; and to put on the new self, created to be like God in true righteousness and holiness. Therefore each of you must put off falsehood and speak truthfully to his neighbor, for we are all members of one body." (Ephesians 4: 22-25)

".......Forgetting what is behind and straining toward what is ahead, I press on toward the goal to win the prize for which God has called me heavenward in Christ Jesus." (Philippians 3:13- 14)

The Worship of Other Gods

"When you have eaten and are satisfied, praise the Lord your God for the good land he has given you." (Deuteronomy 8:10)

"If you ever forget the Lord your God and follow other gods and worship and bow down to them, I testify against you today that you will surely be destroyed. Like the nations the Lord destroyed before you, so you will be destroyed for not obeying the Lord your God." (Deuteronomy 8:19 & 20)

"Fear the Lord your God and serve him. Hold fast to him and take your oaths in his name. He is your praise; he is your God, who performed for you those great and awesome wonders you saw with your own eyes." (Deuteronomy 10: 20 & 21)

"The earth is the Lord's, and everything in it, the world and all who live in it; for he founded it upon the seas and established it upon the waters. Who may ascend the hill of the Lord? Who may stand in his holy place? He who has clean hands and a pure heart, who does not lift up his soul to an idol or swear by what is false. He will receive blessing from the Lord and vindication from God his Savior." (Psalm 24: 1-5)

Chapter 4

Feeling Good About Yourself

You don't have to shop, or spend money on material things to make you happy, that happiness only lasts a little while. "True happiness" is not based upon what you have in your hands, but is something you can carry in your heart. See a merry heart does you good like a medicine. All you have to do is know who you are in Christ and don't let other people around you bring you down; just smile and walk away if it is a verbal insult. If it results in something physical, use the Word by saying out loud "I rebuke you Satan in Jesus Name."

Say that very firmly and BELIEVING in the words no one will ever come close to you or touch you. You NOW have the "POWER of GOD" on your side, which is the GREATEST POWER in this universe. Be confident with your head held high; people love when they see a person with a lot of confidence in themselves, energy, excitement, and pure joy. Other people will start to want to be around you more because they want some of that pure joy, happiness, and peace that you possess within your heart.

Remember the Lord's perfect peace takes away all concern and fear.

Happiness that consists of a healthy mental attitude, a grateful spirit, a clear conscience, and a heart full of God's life, lasts forever. So let nothing move you. Always give yourselves fully to the work of the Lord, because you know that your labor has not been done in vain.

How to Pray and Be Saved

If you confess with your mouth, "Jesus is Lord," and believe in your heart that God raised Him from the dead you will be saved. For it is with your heart that you believe and are justified, and it is with your mouth that you confess and are saved.

"Those whom I love I rebuke and discipline. So be earnest, and repent. Here I am! I stand at the door and knock. If anyone hears my voice and opens the door, I will come in and eat with him, and he with me." (Revelation 3:19 & 20)

"Give ear and come to Jesus; hear Him, that your soul may live. Then He will make an everlasting covenant with you." (Isaiah 55:3)

"For it is by grace you have been saved, through faith – and this not from yourselves, it is the gift of God – not by works, so that no one can boast. For we are God's workmanship, created in Christ Jesus to do good works, which God prepared in advance for us to do." (Ephesians 2:8–10)

"Rejoice in the Lord always, I will say it again: Rejoice! Let your gentleness be evident to all. The Lord is near. Do not be anxious about anything, but in everything, by prayer and petition, with thanksgiving, present your requests to God. And the peace of God, which transcends all understanding, will guard your hearts and your minds in Christ Jesus."

(Philippians 4:4-7)

"Whatever you have learned or received or heard from me, or seen in me – put it into practice. And the God of peace will be with you." (Philippians 4:9)

Some examples of how you should pray are as follows:

1) "But when you pray, do not be like the hypocrites, for they love to pray standing in the synagogues and on the street corners to be seen by men. I tell you the truth, they have received their reward in full. But when you pray, go into your room, close the door and pray to your Father, who is unseen. Then your Father, who sees what is done in secret, will reward you. And when you pray, do not keep on babbling like pagans, for they think they will be heard because of their many words. Do not be like them, for your Father knows what you need before you ask him.

This, then, is how you should pray:

```
Our Father in heaven, hallowed be your name, your kingdom
come, your will be done on earth as it is in heaven.
Give us today our daily bread.
Forgive us our debts, as we also have forgiven our debtors.
And lead us not into temptation,
But deliver us from the evil one.'

For if you forgive men when they sin against you, your
heavenly Father will also forgive you. But if you do not
forgive men their sins, your Father will not forgive your
sins."
(Matthew 6:6-15)
```

2) Here is another example of a good prayer:

A prayer of David.

"Hear, O Lord, and answer me,
for I am poor and needy.
Guard my life, for I am devoted to you.
You are my God; save your servant who trusts in you.
Have mercy on me, O Lord,
for I call to you all day long.
Bring joy to your servant,
for to you, O Lord, I lift up my soul.

You are forgiving and good,
O Lord, abounding in love to all who call to you.
Hear my prayer, O Lord; listen to my cry for mercy.
In the day of my trouble I will call to you,
for you will answer me.

Among the gods there is none like you,O Lord;
no deeds can compare with yours.
All the nations you have made
will come and worship before you,O Lord;
they will bring glory to your name.
For you are great and do marvelous deeds;
you alone are God.

Teach me your way, O Lord,
and I will walk in your truth;
give me an undivided heart,
that I may fear our name.
I will praise you, o Lord my God, with all my heart;
I will glorify your name forever.
For great is your love toward me;
you have delivered me from the depths of the grave.

```
The arrogant are attacking me, O God;
a band of ruthless men seeks my life -
men without regard for you.
But you, O Lord, are a compassionate and gracious God,
slow to anger, abounding in love and faithfulness.

Turn to me and have mercy on me;
grant your strength to your servant
and save the son of your maidservant.
Give me a sign of your goodness,
that my enemies may see it and be put to shame,
for you, O Lord, have helped me and comforted me."


(Psalm 86:1-17)
```

If You Follow Jesus

"Now when a man works, his wages are not credited to him as a gift, but as an obligation. However, to the man who does not work but trusts God who justifies the wicked, his faith is credited as righteousness." (Romans 4:4-5)

If you want to follow Jesus remember you must put him first, then others second. Not your family first, not your loved ones first, but only your Lord and Savior Jesus Christ FIRST.

Also, when you follow Jesus you must have "faith." People may persecute you and falsely say all kinds of evil against you, but blessed are you. Rejoice and jump for joy, because GREAT is your reward in Heaven.

Know that everywhere you go the Holy Spirit will be there in your hardships. Consider your life worth nothing, but only to finish the race and completing the task the Lord Jesus Christ has given you.

"But store up for yourselves treasures in heaven, where moth and rust do not destroy, and where thieves do not break in and steal. For where your treasure is, there your heart will be also." (Matthew 6:20-21)

Chapter 5

Discipline

"Harsh discipline" does not solve the problem...it only covers up what is wrong. Trying to make harsh discipline be a fear factor; well sometimes kids do not care how much trouble they get into, they embrace it. You see understanding the situation solves the problem, but the person who has the problem has to understand what he or she has done wrong. When dealing with a situation, one must handle it with calmness, gentleness, peace and love. Discipline your child as you would see fit, but do it with "loving discipline." Then probably the child will respond to it in a joyful manner and it will help the child grow in the Spirit.

Also, don't behave like a hypocrite when you experience a bad situation. Don't handle the problem with violence and hate, but rather with understanding and love. Next time a bad situation happens (whether it be a physical or verbal confrontation) go inside yourself and find that dwelling place and ask GOD, "What would Jesus do?" You already know Jesus wouldn't be violent or ignorant, but would do what GOD told Him to do. Remember obstacles aren't placed in your pathway to arrest your progress, but to increase your speed of understanding and applying The

Word to every day life.

Pushing Kids

If a child doesn't want to go to "church" don't make he or she go, they will not learn anything. You are just stuffing material in their brains that they are not ready to comprehend yet. Instead, show your child The Word everyday, read a chapter together, let your child be spontaneous. Let he or she come to Jesus when they want to, then when that happens the doors will be open in the child's heart and the Holy Spirit will take control.

You will start to notice it because the child will have the desire and passion to know more about Jesus and the Almighty Power of GOD. Then the Holy Spirit will teach the child all the things he or she needs to know, because he or she wants to know about GOD more and it won't be forced upon the child. When it says in the Bible we should train a child the way that he or she goes, it's mostly saying be a role model to your children. They see you read the Bible and they will want to read the Bible. If the kids see you acting some way not pleasing in God's eyes, the kids will do the same. "They don't care, they do whatever their parents do." (whether good or bad)

"Be Open & Don't Keep Secrets From Your Children (or they will find out)

Always be able to talk about anything with your children. Do not keep secrets from your children. If they feel you are keeping something from them, then they will start keeping secrets from you. Be open to talk about anything with your children, even if it is something horrible.

Don't ever yell; be calm, cool, collective, gentle, peaceful and loving. Try to understand the situation if it is bad and help the child understand what they did wrong so it will not happen again. Be proud of your children; show that you appreciate them and if they did something good...commend them. Always say, "I love you and I'm proud of you!"

Always encourage your child, by doing this you must let them explore the world (good and bad) and let God take them down the righteous path. If you do not give your children the freedom and your trust, they are going to be curious about it anyway and when they grow up they are going to do whatever the parents told them not to do. Don't hide knowledge from your children; let your children know what the world is all about. If you don't and shield them too much, they will not be prepared when they see a whole different world from when they were children.

Different Kinds of Families

People think a normal family has to be a Mom and Dad with a child. It doesn't have to be like that, there is no such thing as a normal family (In GOD's eyes). It can consist of friends being "God sisters and God brothers."

A "true family" can be as big as you want it or as small as you want it. The MOST important factor is that the family consist of people who you love and who love and care about you as much as you do them...thus having a positive influence on one another. A positive influence is seen in a case of an individual who cares about Jesus and talks about Him daily, with TRUE enthusiasm and PURE JOY!!! He or she is always being positive when everything around the individual seems negative. When you surround yourself around those types of people, you will become a happier person...that is a "true family."

If you want a father or mother figure, let God be the one to fill that space. For God is the soul's lover, the soul's friend, father, mother, brother, sister...etc. Remember "true family" isn't about whose blood you have, it is about who you TRULY LOVE and care about from the heart. For God created us all.

For Jesus says in Mark 3:35: "Whoever does God's will is my brother and sister and mother."

The Day Is Near

"....... The hour has come for you to wake up from your slumber, because our salvation is nearer now than when we first believed. The night is nearly over; the day is almost here. So let us put aside the deeds of darkness and put on the armor of light. Let us behave decently, as in the daytime, not in orgies and drunkenness, not in sexual immorality and debauchery, not in dissension and jealousy. Rather, clothe yourselves with the Lord Jesus Christ, and do not think about how to gratify the desires of the human nature." (Romans 13:11-14)

"When anyone hears the message about the kingdom and does not understand it, the evil one comes and snatches away what was sown in his heart. This is the seed sown along the path. The one who received the seed that fell on rocky places is the man who hears the word and at once receives it with joy. But since he has no root, he lasts only a short time. When trouble or persecution comes because of the word, he quickly falls away. The one who received the seed that fell among the thorns is the man who hears the word, but the worries of this life and the deceitfulness of wealth choke it, making it unfruitful. But the one who received the seed that fell on good soil is the man who hears the word and understands it. He produces a crop, yielding a hundred, sixty or thirty times what was sown." (Matthew 13:19-23)

"...Maintain justice and do what is right, for my salvation is close at hand and my righteousness will soon be revealed." (Isaiah 56:1)

"The Sovereign Lord declares that the days are coming when He will send a famine through the land—not a famine of food or a thirst for water, but a famine of hearing the words of the Lord." (Amos 8:11)

"Brothers, we do not want you to be ignorant about those who fall asleep, or to grieve like the rest of the men, who have no hope. We believe that Jesus died and rose again and so we believe that God will bring with Jesus those who have fallen asleep in him. According to the Lord's own word, we tell you that we who are still alive, who are left till the coming of the Lord, will certainly not precede those who have fallen asleep. For the Lord himself will come down from heaven, with a loud command, with the voice of the archangel and with the trumpet call of God, and the dead in Christ will rise first. After that, we who are still alive and are left will be caught up together with them in the clouds to meet the Lord in the air. And so we will be with the Lord forever." (1 Thessalonians 4:13-17)

"The end of all things is near. Therefore be clear minded and self-controlled so that you can pray. Above all, love each other deeply, because love covers over a multitude of sins. Offer hospitality to one another without grumbling. Each one should use whatever gift he has received to serve others, faithfully administering God's grace in its various forms. If anyone speaks, he should do it as one speaking the very words of God. If anyone serves, he should do it with the strength God provides, so that in all things God may be praised through Jesus Christ. To him be the glory and the power for ever and ever. Amen." (1 Peter 4:7-11)

"The good man brings good things out of the good stored up in him, and the evil man brings evil things out of the evil stored up in him. But I tell you that men will have to give account on the Day of Judgment for every careless word they have spoken. For by your words you will be acquitted, and by your words you will be condemned." (Matthew 12:35-37)

In the land, there is no faithfulness, no love, and no acknowledgment of God. There is only cursing, lying, murder, stealing and adultery. The days of punishment are coming; the days of reckoning are at hand. But He is a gracious and compassionate God; slow to anger and abounding in love, a God who relents from sending calamity. He is forgiving in sin and rebellion, but he does not leave the guilty unpunished. So fear the Lord and serve Him with all faithfulness.

To those who have already served faithfully this is what the Lord says, "Since you have kept my command to endure patiently, I will also keep you from the hour of trial that is gong to come upon the whole world to test those who live on the earth. I am coming soon. Hold on to what you have, so that no one will take your crown. Him who overcomes I will make a pillar in the temple of my God. Never again will he leave it. I will write on him the name of my God and the name of the city of my God, the new Jerusalem, which is coming down out of heaven from my God; and I will also write on him my new name." (Revelation 3:10-12)

"Let us therefore make every effort to do what leads to peace and to mutual edification." (Romans 14:19)

May the God of peace be with you all. Amen.

<u>ABOUT THE AUTHOR:</u>

Website: https://thetruth32.com

Instagram: Brandon_Alfred5

ASPIRING THERAPIST